Sports Safety

BY ELIZABETH LANG

The Child's World

Published by The Child's World®
1980 Lookout Drive • Mankato, MN 56003-1705
800-599-READ • www.childsworld.com

Acknowledgments
The Child's World®: Mary Berendes, Publishing Director
Red Line Editorial: Editorial direction
The Design Lab: Design
Amnet: Production
Photographs ©: Front cover: PhotoDisc; ComStock; PhotoDisc,
2, 6, 15; ComStock, 3, 4, 14, 18; BrandX Pictures, 5, 11, 16, 19; Kids in
Motion, 7, 17; Tatyana Vychegzhanina/Shutterstock Images,
9, 21 (top left); Majoros GÃ¡bor/Shutterstock Images, 10, 23; shutswis/
Shutterstock Images, 12, 21 (bottom left); Yarek Gora/Shutterstock
Images, 13; Kitch Bain/Shutterstock Images, 13, 21 (right)

ISBN: 978-1623235413
LCCN: 2013931340

Printed in the United States of America
Mankato, MN
July, 2013
PA02174

ABOUT THE AUTHOR

Elizabeth Lang is a writer and teacher. She lives in Olympia, Washington, with her husband, three children, three cats, two dogs, and a great deal of rain.

Table of Contents

CHAPTER ONE

Play It Safe

What a day. Just when you broke your speed record, your skateboard skidded on a rock and launched you into a cement wall. Then, a gigantic bug flew in your eye while you were riding your bike. During your baseball game, you were playing catcher and the batter missed the ball. It walloped you in the chest. To top it all off, it was a scorching 100 degrees outside! Could your day have been any worse?

Yes, much worse, because you had protection. Your helmet, eyewear, chest protector, and water bottle got you through the day. They might have even saved your life. That's what sports safety is all about!

▼ *Wearing a helmet while riding your bike helps you avoid injuries.*

► *Millions of kids play team sports such as football.*

Do you play sports? If so, you're not alone. About 41 million American children and teenagers play a sport outside of school. While sports are great for your health, they do put you at risk for injury. According to the Centers for Disease Control and Prevention, about 2.6 million children and teens are treated for sports injuries in hospital emergency rooms every year.

◄ *Many doctors say that playing sports is good for you, even though there's a chance you may be injured.*

But that does not mean you should not play sports. Many doctors who treat injured athletes say that playing sports is so good for you, it is better to take the risk of injury than to not play at all. Besides, there are many things you can do to stay out of the emergency room.

One of the easiest ways to avoid injury is to stay fit all year round. Practicing a sport puts strain on your muscles. If you go from being a couch potato to being the pitcher for your baseball team, you will have a weak arm. A weak arm can be easily injured. Stay active all year to avoid injuring yourself during your sports season.

Another way to avoid injury is to stretch. Have you ever watched a cat stretch? How about a dog? Even a bird will stretch its wings to warm up its **joints**. If the animals are doing it, why not you? **Flexibility** is how well you move your joints and muscles. Staying flexible helps avoid injury and pain. If you are stiff from having ridden a horse all day and you try to do the splits, it is

▶ *Stretching helps your muscles become more flexible and avoid injury.*

probably going to hurt. You might even get injured. Stretching increases flexibility. Without stretching, **tendons**, **ligaments**, and muscles will shorten. Over time, this can cause damage.

Before you stretch, make sure you warm up your body. Get your blood pumping with a light jog, some jumping jacks, or even skipping. Then try these stretches. Hold each stretch for 15 to 30 seconds.

Neck: Sit or stand with your shoulders relaxed and your back straight. Bend your right ear down toward your right shoulder and hold. Now roll your head down toward the ground so that your chin is above your chest. Hold it. Now roll your head to the left and bring that ear to your left shoulder. Remember to breathe throughout the exercise.

Thighs: Stand with your feet hip width apart. You may want to hold onto a chair for balance. Keep your back straight. Lift your left foot behind

CAT, CAMEL, EAGLE, AND BUTTERFLY

Yoga is a practice that started over 3,000 years ago in India. Yoga improves flexibility, strength, and balance. It can be fun for kids because it uses animal poses to get you warmed up. The "cat and camel" pose stretches your back. The "butterfly" pose stretches your hips, and the "eagle" pose stretches your upper body.

you until you can reach back and grab your foot with your left hand. Keep your thighs next to each other. Do not pull your left thigh back behind you. Repeat with your right leg.

Upper Arms: Stand with your left elbow in your right hand. Reach your left arm over your head while holding your elbow in your right hand. Try to reach your left fingertips down your spine. Now repeat with your other arm.

▶ *Stretching helps your muscles warm up before playing sports.*

CHAPTER TWO

Gear Up!

Protective gear is what you wear to help keep you safe. When it comes to sports, the kind of gear you will need depends on what you are playing.

There is a reason adults tell you to put on your helmet. Helmets prevent brain injuries and can save your life. There are different helmets for different sports. Whichever one you choose, the helmet needs to fit snuggly. Make sure you are wearing the right helmet before riding your bike, skateboarding, and in-line skating. Also, put a helmet on before playing football, hockey, baseball, softball, or other sports that may cause head injuries.

Injuries to the eyes are the leading cause of blindness for kids in the United States. Sports cause

▲ *Helmets protect your brain from being injured.*

▶ *Opposite page: Football players wear helmets to protect their heads from injury.*

many of them. The lenses of most protective eyewear are made of a special material that is ten times stronger than plastic. Goggles and safety glasses can look cool, too. Pick out your favorite style before playing baseball, basketball, hockey, racquetball, or softball. Wear goggles or safety glasses before going bicycling, downhill skiing, or snowboarding.

Mouth guards protect your mouth, tongue, and teeth when you play. Dental injuries are common in sports. However, they can easily be prevented. Mouth guards make sure your teeth do not get knocked out, broken, or chipped. Here are just a few sports where you will want a mouth guard: gymnastics, basketball, hockey, football, lacrosse, volleyball, surfing, soccer, and martial arts.

Other safety gear protects your joints. Wrist, knee, and elbow pads can prevent arm and wrist **fractures**. Knee guards can protect you from cuts

▼ *Wear goggles to protect your eyes when you ski or snowboard.*

GEAR ISN'T JUST FOR SPORTS!
If you think it is a pain to wear *your* gear, think about firefighters. By the time a firefighter has on boots, a coat, a helmet, turnout pants, a face mask, a radio, a flashlight, a hood, and an ax, he or she has added 60 pounds of weight! Firefighters also carry special cameras to detect heat, and they sometimes carry a hose. Does your helmet still seem heavy?

Mouth guards protect your teeth in team sports such as lacrosse.

Drink lots of water to stay hydrated at practice or during a game.

and bruises. Slip on protective pads before you skateboard, ride a scooter, roller skate, or in-line skate.

Do not forget your water bottle! As you play, your muscles make heat inside you and your body temperature riscs. When you get hot, you sweat. When the sweat dries, it cools you down. It is good to sweat—your body is doing its job. But if you do not replace the fluids you lose from sweating by drinking water, you can get **dehydrated**. Being dehydrated can make you weak, tired, dizzy, and sick to your stomach.

When you are swinging a bat or kicking a ball for hours, it is easy to get sunburned. That's why it is important that you protect your skin with sunscreen. Put on sunscreen 15 to 20 minutes before going outside, and reapply every two hours. Wear a hat with a brim to protect your face from the sun's rays.

▼ *Wear a brimmed hat such as this one when you play baseball to protect your face and eyes from the sun.*

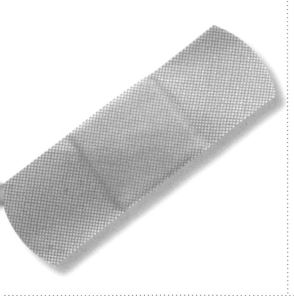

▼ *It's common to get cuts and scrapes while playing sports.*

CHAPTER THREE

When It Hurts

There is a saying, "No pain, no gain." It means if you do not feel pain while exercising, you must not be working hard enough. But this is not the way to play safely. Pay attention if you feel hurt. Any pain that gets worse with playing or causes swelling should be seen by a doctor.

Your fingers, arms, and legs are not the only body parts that can get hurt during sports. Your head, neck, and back can suffer serious sports injuries, too. If you feel pain anywhere on your body while playing a sport, tell your coach or another adult!

You should get injuries to your head checked by a doctor. A **concussion** is an injury to the brain caused by a blow to the head. It may not be life

► Doing gymnastics can cause neck injuries.

threatening, but it can cause problems. If you get a concussion, you may feel confused, have a headache, feel sick to your stomach, and even briefly lose **consciousness**. Most people heal from one concussion with no long-term problems. But each time you have a concussion, it is easier to get another one. Repeated concussions can damage your brain.

Sports injuries can also affect your neck. One injury to the neck is called *whiplash*. It happens when your head has been forcefully jerked. It causes a stinging burn that comes from stretching the nerves in your neck. Most neck injuries are caused by a

◄ Opposite page: Always see a doctor when your head's been injured while playing sports.

blow to the head or by falling. But your neck can also be injured little by little over time. Neck injuries sometimes happen in sports such as horseback riding, diving, judo, or gymnastics.

Playing sports can also cause back injuries. Backs can get bruised, fractured, and sprained. Back injuries can be caused by twisting, such as in gymnastics, or from a blow when playing **contact sports** such as football and hockey. The lower back—the part of your spine down by your waist—usually gets hurt more often than your upper back, because it twists and bends as you play. But the upper back—the middle part of your spine by your ribs—can also get hurt in sports. Sports that require you to rotate your shoulders, such as swimming or tennis, can cause upper-back injuries.

Most sports injuries are painful but not serious. Strains or sprains in a **limb** are more common

▼ *Swimming can cause injuries to your upper back.*

RICE IT!

To treat a sprain, follow these steps:

Rest the injured area.

Ice it for 15 minutes. Use a cold pack or wrap the ice in a towel before putting it on your skin.

Compress the injury. This means to firmly wrap the injured area with an elastic bandage. Compressing reduces pain caused by swelling.

Elevate, or raise, the injured area above your heart. This helps with swelling by draining fluid from the **tissue**.

▶ *Cheering from the sidelines is fun, and resting helps your injuries heal.*

than concussions and whiplash. A strain is when a muscle has been stretched too far. A sprain is when a ligament has been stretched too far, or worse, torn.

Now that you know how to protect yourself and what to do if you are injured, here comes the hard part—sitting out. If you get hurt while playing and do not give your injury a good rest, it could get worse. So rest up, cheer your team on from the sidelines, and then get back out there.

Hands-on Activity:
Take the Egg Challenge!

What You'll Need:

Hard-boiled eggs, cardboard box, garbage bag, soft materials of your choice

Directions:

1. First, think of a way to drop one of the eggs into the box from a height of 3 feet (1 m). You could roll it off a couch, build a ramp, or simply drop it.

2. Then, line the box with the garbage bag. Put any material you want in the box (such as shredded paper or cotton balls) so the egg does not crack when it falls into the box.

3. Next, think of a way to package the egg so that it will survive the fall when the box has no material in it.

4. Finally, drop the egg into the box using the methods you created. Did it crack? You can try different ways to protect the eggs and see which one works the best.

5. Now, think of sports where people might fall to the ground or get hit by balls. How are they protected from injury?

SPORTS SAFETY

Glossary

concussion (kun-KUSH-un): A concussion is an injury to the brain. You may get a concussion when you are hit in the head while playing a sport.

consciousness (KON-chus-nis): Consciousness is the state of being aware of your surroundings, senses, and thoughts. Having consciousness means you are awake.

contact sports (KON-takt sports): Contact sports are sports that involve body contact between two opposing players. Football and hockey are contact sports.

dehydrated (dee-HYE-dreyt-id): Being dehydrated happens when your body loses more fluids than it takes in. If you do not drink water when playing sports, you can get dehydrated.

flexibility (FLEKS-uh-bil-uh-tee): Flexibility is how well you move your joints and muscles. Stretch to improve your flexibility.

fractures (FRAK-shurz): Fractures are the breaking of bones. Fractures may occur in contact sports such as football and hockey.

joints (joynts): Joints are the places where two bones come together. Your elbows and knees are joints.

ligaments (LIG-uh-mints): Ligaments are bands of tissues that connect bones together and hold organs in place. Stretching can help keep your ligaments from shortening.

limb (lim): A limb is one of a human's arms or legs. Fractures and sprains can happen to a limb.

tendons (TEN-dunz): Tendons are bands of thick, tough tissues that connect muscle to bone. Stretching keeps your tendons from getting shorter, which causes damage.

tissue (TISH-yoo): Tissue is made up of groups of cells that perform the same function in your body. Sprains may injure tissue.

To Learn More

BOOKS

Berman, Len. *And Nobody Got Hurt 2! The World's Weirdest, Wackiest, and Most Amazing True Sports Stories.* New York: Little, Brown, and Co., 2007.

Wiese, Jim. *Sports Science: 40 Goal-Scoring, High-Flying, Medal-Winning Experiments for Kids.* New York: John Wiley & Sons, Inc., 2002.

WEB SITES

Visit our Web site for links about sports safety: **childsworld.com/links**

Note to Parents, Teachers, and Librarians: We routinely verify our Web links to make sure they are safe and active sites. So encourage your readers to check them out!

Index